Rhyming Riddles and Tons of Tongue Twisters for Miles of Smiles

By

Edith Namm

This book is a work of fiction. Places, events, and situations in this story are purely fictional. Any resemblance to actual persons, living or dead, is coincidental.

© 2002 by Edith Namm. All rights reserved.

No part of this book may be reproduced, stored in a retrieval system, or transmitted by any means, electronic, mechanical, photocopying, recording, or otherwise, without written permission from the author.

ISBN: 1-4033-5852-4 (e-book)
ISBN: 1-4033-5853-2 (Paperback)

This book is printed on acid free paper.

1stBooks - rev. 01/29/03

Dedicated to Children of all Ages and Stages
And to their Parents

For Free, Friendly, Family Fun

RHYMING RIDDLES AND TONS OF TONGUE TWISTERS celebrates the joy of Smiles and Laughter. Its fun-filled pages have the power to positively energize a Reader's Mind and Body and generate miles of Smiles and Laughter.

Happy Feelings, Smiles, and Laughter supply One's Mind and Body with the Positive Energy that is needed to feel good about One's Self.

ABOUT THE POWER OF LAUGHTER AND SMILES

Laughter is the most inexpensive and most effective wonder drug.

Laughter is a universal medicine.

Bertrand Russell

Laughter is the shortest distance between 2 People.

Victor Borge

Laughter is free, legal, has no calories, no cholesterol, no preservatives, no artificial ingredients and is absolutely safe.

Dale Irvin

Laughter

Gives your Heart and Diaphragm Muscles a beneficial workout.

Improves your Circulation.

Fills your Lungs with oxygen-rich air.

Clears your Respiratory Passages.

Stimulates the release of Endorphins (Good Feeling Hormones) into your Bloodstream.

Reduces the tension in your Central Nervous System.

A Smile is a curve that sets everything straight.
Phyllis Diller

A Smile relaxes your Facial Muscles, softens your Frown Lines, and acts as a Natural Face Lift.

To increase your Positive Energy Power and relieve any Sad, Anxious, Angry Feelings and Thoughts, I highly recommend a Mile of Smiles and Laughs as a daily exercise.

Read and accurately say each Tongue Twister 3 times as fast as you can. Increase your speed and accuracy for all Tongue Twisters. Memorize any favorite Tongue Twisters.

For a natural facelift, say your favorite memorized Tongue Twisters as many times as necessary until a frown turns into a smile.

When you want Anger, Sadness, Doubt and Fear to disappear, say your favorite memorized Tongue Twisters as many times as necessary until a smile appears.

For pleasant dreams, say your favorite memorized Tongue Twisters before going to sleep.

To have a great day, say your favorite memorized Tongue Twisters upon waking.

To increase your Smile Mileage, place Yellow Smiling Face Stickers everywhere to serve as a reminder to Smile. Smile every time you look into the mirror!!!

To Feel Good, seek to be with people who have Positive Energy Power. You can always tell a Person with Positive Energy Power by the smile that he/she is wearing.

CONTENTS

RHYMING RIDDLES 1
  WHAT AM I? 1
  ANSWERS TO RHYMING RIDDLES—WHAT AM I?
  19
  WHAT"S MY NAME? 20
  ANSWERS TO RHYMING RIDDLES—WHAT'S MY NAME? 29

RHYMING WORDS 31

TONS OF TONGUE TWISTERS FOR MILES OF SMILES 43

OTHER BOOKS WRITTEN BY EDITH NAMM. 91

Rhyming Riddles and Tons of Tongue Twisters for Miles of Smiles

RHYMING RIDDLES

WHAT AM I?

I am never in the sea
I never drink tea
I am a _____ .

I never float
In a boat
With a coat
I am a _____ .

I am long
I am strong
I eat till I am full
I am a _____ .

Edith Namm

Only in water, do I wish
To swish
I am a _____ .

I fail to deliver mail
I prefer to go for a sail
I am a _____ .

Never a sound will you hear
When I am near
I steer clear
Of any sound I hear
I am a _____ .

As a stuffed pet
I am all set
To share and care
I am a _____ .

I am not comfortable on a log
I am a _____.

I don't eat pork
With a fork
I am a _____.

I can never fit into a box
I am not an ox
I am a _____.

Edith Namm

I am never in a park
I am quite dark
I do not bark
I am a _____.

I have no cane
I have no mane
I am not a plane
I am a _____.

I can grab
I am drab
I am a _____.

I am frail
I am as thin as a rail
I have a tail
I never wail
I am not a nail
I do not care for a pail
I leave a trail
I am a _____.

To hop is my habit
I am a _____.

I wiggle and squirm
I am a _____.

Edith Namm

At night, I hoot and howl
I am an _____ .

I gallop with force
On any course
I am a _____ .

I don't take much space
I am fast in a race
I love a warm house
I am a _____ .

Rhyming Riddles and Tons of Tongue Twisters for Miles of Smiles

I am not fat
I never need a hat
I am a _____.

I get by
High in the sky
I am a _____.

Edith Namm

I can not carry a load
You can see me on the road
I am a _____ .

Many will flee
Few are filled with glee
When they see me
I am a _____ .

Rarely, do I have the luck
To ride in a truck
I am a _____.

To satisfy my curiosity
I always look for the key
I am a _____.

Edith Namm

I never get a hug
I am just a little _____.

You can see me on a log
You can see me in a fog
You can see me in a smog
You will never see me jog
I am a _____.

I am big
I do not care to dig
I do not care for a fig
I do not care for a twig
I never wear a wig
I am a _____.

I am a cell
I may have some jell
I can not smell
I can not spell
I can not yell
I am a _____.

Edith Namm

		I come in every shape and size
		I never go to bed
		I always have to rise
		I never wear the color red
		I am a _____.

		I twinkle and shine
		Only from afar
		I am a _____.

Rhyming Riddles and Tons of Tongue Twisters for Miles of Smiles

I bring cheer and fun
I am the _____.

You never see me at noon
You never see me with a spoon
I am the _____.

I bounce small
I bounce tall
I bounce anywhere at all
In a hall
Against a wall
I am a _____.

Edith Namm

       I am not in a lake
       I am not a fake
       To make
       Please bake
       Take care not to shake
       I am a _____ .

       I take people near and far
       I am a _____ .

Rhyming Riddles and Tons of Tongue Twisters for Miles of Smiles

I have no leg
On which to stand
Or land
I am just an _____.

I have a tone
I have a drone
I help when you are alone
I am not made of stone
I am a _____.

Edith Namm

        I do not knock
        I do not lock
        I am not good in a sock
        I am a _____ .

        I do not sit
        I do not flit
        I do not hit
        I do not quit
        I do not slit
        I do not spit
        I am a _____ .

I am rarely bent
I rarely have a dent
I can be lent
I can be spent
I can be sent
I have no scent
I am a _____.

I can not walk
I can not talk
I can not balk
I am _____.

Edith Namm

I am not a fin
I am not a pin
I am made of skin
I am at the bottom of a grin
I am a _____.

Rhyming Riddles and Tons of Tongue Twisters for Miles of Smiles

ANSWERS TO RHYMING RIDDLES
WHAT AM I?

Flea	Bee
Goat	Duck
Bull	Monkey
Fish	Bug
Whale	Frog
Deer	Pig
Bear	Shell
Dog	Bread
Stork	Star
Fox	Sun
Shark	Moon
Crane	Ball
Crab	Cake
Snail	Car
Rabbit	Egg
Worm	Phone
Owl	Rock
Horse	Pit
Mouse	Cent
Cat	Chalk
Fly	Chin
Toad	

Edith Namm

WHAT"S MY NAME?

I am brave
I save and save
My name is _____.

I love jam
I love ham
I love a yam
I'm not so sure about a clam
My name is _____.

Rhyming Riddles and Tons of Tongue Twisters for Miles of Smiles

I am not a crank
I play no prank
My name is _____.

I love to eat a banana
My name is _____.

Sometimes we can be silly
Our names are _____, _____,
_____.

Edith Namm

I love to bounce a ball
Any place or time at all
Just call
My name is _____.

I love to skate
I am never late
I eat whatever is on my plate
My name is _____.

We are hardly ever sick
Our names are _____.

I believe you have to tell the truth
My name is _____.

I stand straight as a rail
My name is _____.

Edith Namm

      To us, nothing is scary
      Our   names   are   _____,
  _____, _____.

      We are well fed
      We know when to go to bed
      We love the color red
      Our names are _____,
  _____, _____.

We're slim and trim
We're full of vim
We love to swim
Our names are _____,
_____, _____.

To be cool, I use a fan
I try everything I can
My name is _____.

Edith Namm

Wherever I go
I am easily seen
My name is _____.

With my hands, I'm mighty handy
My name is _____.

I can never be as light as a feather
My name is _____.

I'll give you a clue
I love the color blue
My name is _____.

Edith Namm

I am a boy
Full of joy
My name is _____.

Rhyming Riddles and Tons of Tongue Twisters for Miles of Smiles

ANSWERS TO RHYMING RIDDLES—WHAT'S MY NAME?

Dave

Pam

Frank

Anna

Billy, Milly, Willy

Paul

Kate

Nick, Rick

Ruth

Edith Namm

    Gail
    Barry, Gary, Harry, Larry

    Ed, Fred, Ned, Ted

    Jim, Kim, Tim

    Ann

    Jean

    Andy

    Heather

    Sue

    Roy

RHYMING WORDS

A fat cat sat on a flat mat.

A rat scats when it sees a cat.

Can you grab the crab that's on the drab slab?

Karl said the jar is not in the car and is not on the bar.

A small ball hit the tall wall in the mall hall.

Brad was glad he had seen Chad's Dad.

Tap the cap of the chap with a map on his lap.

Stack the snacks in the black backpack that is on the rack in the shack

The man ran into the van for a pan of bran and a tan fan.

The bland band was banned from the grandstand.

The champ had a cramp on the damp, camp ramp.

Ben has his ten wrens in a pen when Ken has his ten hens in the den.

Ted and Fred fled from the shed with a red sled, while well-fed Ned sped to bed.

The man lent Kent a bent tent.

Tell Mel a bell fell into the well and caused the well to smell.

Rhyming Riddles and Tons of Tongue Twisters for Miles of Smiles

Kim, Jim, and Tim swim to be slim and trim.

A chill caused Will and Jill to feel ill.

Can you grip the tip of a chip with your lip?

In a fog or smog, can you see a hog or a frog jog on a log?

Edith Namm

The tot did not spot the hot pot.

A hound is bound to pound a mound on the ground.

Rub and scrub the cub in the tub.

Bake and take a cake to Jake.

Can a quake shake the fake snake near the lake?

State the rate of the plate on the crate near the gate.

Kate was late for the date with her mate.

Drain the rain from the grain that is on the plain.
A strain and a sprain caused a pain in his brain.

Gail failed to see a frail snail in the pail.

Gail waited in the rain to hail the mail train.

A nail in the quail's tail made the quail wail.

Hail the snail that can sail on a rail.

She paid the maid to braid the suede shade.

This is the place for the space race.

Kneel to feel the steel wheel with your heel.

Bea said she saw a bee flee with glee from her knee.

A meal of veal makes a real seal squeal with zeal.

Did Ned need to feed the steed standing on the sturdy stony stand?

Lyle saw piles of files and miles of tiles.

Might the sight of a bright night light frighten a child?

Did Sy spy a sly fly try to fly in the sky?

A coy toy brought joy to the boy.

Harold was told to hold the old gold mold.

Edith Namm

Oil can spoil the soil.

A volt jolt made the colt bolt.

TONS OF TONGUE TWISTERS FOR MILES OF SMILES

Andy, Annie, and Alex applauded the agile arctic animals' amazing aquatic acts.

A high altitude altered Allen's attitude.

An allergic ape ate all the assorted autumn apples and avoided the appealing amber apricots.

Edith Namm

Alice, Al, and Allie are all in awe of an awl in the alley.

Amy aims to aid an aging, ailing ape.

The bored boar broke the broad, black board.

The bold brown baby bear bounced on the barren bench and burst a bunch of bright blue balloons.

Betty's biscuit batter was bitter.

Bert bit a bit of a bitter bit
If Bert bit a bit of a bitter bit, where's the bit of the bitter bit that Bert bit?

The busy beaver dug a big black broad burrow.

Better let a busy, buzzing bee be.

Ben's brave, burly burro budged the boat's big black barrels.

Brad's braying burro burrows big baskets of buttered biscuits.

Did the bowler bowl a bowl in the ballroom?
If the bowler bowled a bowl in the ballroom where's the bowl the bowler bowled?

Carrie carried the cute, coy cat to the clean camp cabin.

The chubby, chunky chimp chose to chase the calm camel.

The callous crouching cat caught a curious, creeping, crawling caterpillar.

The creative clown coaxed the clumsy crocodile into the clear, cold creek.

Can Connie close the closest clothes closet?

Crystal caught the clean, clear, crystal cup.
If Crystal caught the clean, clear, crystal cup, where's the clean, clear crystal cup that Crystal caught?

The determined duo decided to discard the dull disks.
If the determined duo decided to discard the dull disks, where are the dull disks the determined duo decided to discard?

Dean delivered a delightfully decorated doll to the doctor's delightful daughter.

Drew drew a dozen dandy dancing deer on a dry, drab door.

The dynamic dragon danced with the delighted dinosaur in the dusty, distant, dry desert.

The daring dove dived down into a deep, dark bush.

Do you desire dozens of daily delicious desserts?
If you do desire dozens of daily delicious desserts, where are the dozens of daily delicious desserts you desire?

The determined dirty dog dug dozens of deep, dark ditches.

Energetic Elliot elects to eat eight edible eggs every evening.

Energetic Ernest excels by exercising in earnest.

Eighteen enormous elephants entertained 88 enthusiastic elves.

Forty-five frail foxes foraged for food.

Frank has fifty favorite, faithful, furry friends.

Fran filmed the funny, frisky filly.

A few fiery fireflies flew from the flue.

The frisky frog found 55 feisty fleas and flies.

The flounder flipped, flopped, and floundered on the firm flat floor.

The fledgling fluttered its fine flight feathers.

Did the flare from the flame fizzle out?

Frank found a file to file the five file drawers.

The fine felt that Fran felt, felt fine.

See Bea for three free freebies.

If flies fly, do fleas flee?

Fifty festive flags fly on friendly Fred's famous farm.

Edith Namm

The grumpy, gray goat glared at the good-natured gorilla.

Glen giggles as he goes to grip the gallery gavel.

The gigantic giraffe galloped to the green, glossy grass.

Gary gave Grace a graceful, golden goose.

Rhyming Riddles and Tons of Tongue Twisters for Miles of Smiles

Did Greta graciously greet the glamorous guests?
If Greta graciously greeted the glamorous guests, where are the glamorous guests that Greta graciously greeted?

Did the groggy graduate gradually grind the green grain on the grassy ground?
If the groggy graduate gradually ground the green grain on the grassy ground, where's the green grain the groggy graduate gradually ground on the grassy ground?

Harry hosed the huge hornet hovering over the hare's hairy head.

Helpful Hannah handed the hoarse horse healthy honey.

Does Hugh have a heavy hoe to hoe a hollow hole?

Healthy humor helps Heath have happy, high hopes.

Has Harvey hastened to hire hearty Harry to help him haul the heavy ham to his house?

The intelligent inventor invented an important, impressive, incredible invention.

Ilene's illustration included icy icicles, igloos, and icebergs on an icy isolated island.

John jostled the jubilant jogger.

Jim just got jam on Jan's jade jacket.

Jan jabbed and jiggled the jagged jammed jamb.

The jittery junior jogger jumped for joy at the jester's jokes.

The jovial juggler juggled juice jars and jugs.

Jack saw a jumbo jet jackal jumping in the jungle.

Kevin kept the curious kitten in a clean kennel.

Kim and Ken know not who knotted the knotty knot.

Kate cooked kale in a copper kettle.
If Kate cooked kale in a copper kettle, where's the kale that Kate cooked?

Lilly lingered to look at the little lamb's limber limb.

Edith Namm

The last lively lark landed on a large leaky launch landing.

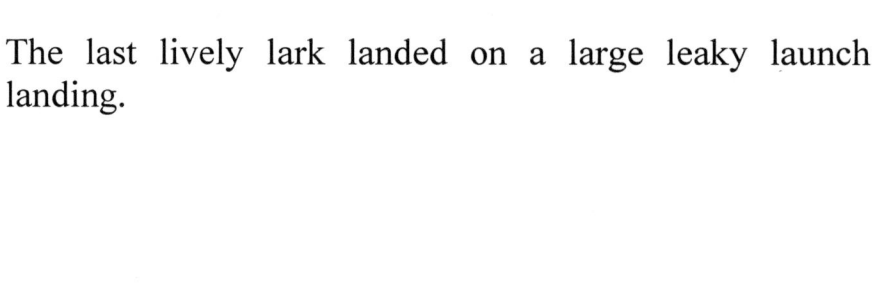

Lara laughed at the large lion's little, light, leathery leash.

Did Luke lift the latter ladder?
If Luke lifted the latter ladder, where's the latter ladder that Luke lifted?

Let us look at the lively lamb lunching on leafy lettuce.

Larry and Lisa lost the last, long, legal letter.

The lonely lady likes to look at the lively lizards leaning on the low, long, log landing.

Lilly loves lovely large lilies.

Lenny went left when he left.

Edith Namm

Lyle likes to lean on the long lean lamp-post.

The maid made many man-made magic magnets.
If the maid made many man-made magic magnets, where are the many magic man-made magnets the maid made?

The Marshal made a million mighty men march many muddy miles on the marsh in March.

Did the male manager manage to mail the mail in the mall?

Does the main male mallard have a mane?

Did the mare mar the modern metallic machine?

Edith Namm

Mel met Matt's massive male mastiff mascot.

May may have a measly meager main meal.

Did the miller mill millet in the mill?
If the miller milled millet in the mill, where's the millet the miller milled?

Do mussels have muscles?
If mussels have muscles, where are the muscles that mussels have?

Mark's magic marker made many marker marks on Mark's mother's marble mantle.

Did Max make mousse for the mouse and the moose? If Max made mousse for the mouse and the moose, where's the mousse that Max made?

Many mischievous monkeys made a massive mound in the muddy meadow.

A moderate mod mode is a modest model's motto.

Noel noticed Nick nibbling on ninety-nine nourishing natural nuts.

Noah's nose knows when it is time to eat.

Nat is not a nervous novice.

One old otter offered the other old otter one ounce of oily oats.

The odd odor overwhelmed the overwrought owner.

Owen offered the old obese orangutan one oversized orange.

Place the pair of pared pears in the pale pink pail.

A pair of plain platform planks made a perfect parallel pattern.

Pam placed a pan of pasty pasta on the paved park path for the prized pet possum and the perky prickly porcupine.

The peppy pair prepared a peppery pepper pot pie for the preppy party.

Paul papered the plain pale painted wall with pretty patterned paper.

Pete's pudgy prancing puppy paused to play with his paws.

Perry and Pearl plan to plant and prune poplars in the popular park.

The patient practitioner praised the patient's patience.

The pleasant parrot preened the pleased parakeet.

Pat prefers paddling a paddle to pedaling a piddling pedal.

Preston presently proposes to present a practical present to the President.

The prior printer printed the principal's principle prime primer.

Paul pledged to pitch plenty of pecans to the placid plump pink pig.

Penny plans to plant plenty of poppy plants in plain plastic planters.

Pam planned to pass the pass past Pat.

Pearl picked, prepared and packed a peachy peach pie for the picnic.

The proud peacock paused to peer at the passive pelican's poised posture on the pier.

The pensive penguin is permitted to perch on the plain platform plank.

The quiet, queasy quail quit quivering.

The Queen questioned the questionable quoted quotient.

The quorum quit quibbling over the quarterly quota.

Quincy quickly quaffed a quarter of a quart of milk.

Rick returned the rickety, rusty rake to the rustic, rural rear room.

A restless ram rambled on to the rough, rocky ranch ramp.

Ray was recruited to record the rare record.

Riley really remembered to remind Ray to remove the ragged, rancid rags from the red reef.

Ralph recommended the ruby red radio remote be removed and replaced.

The rancher rescued a rabbit from the restless ravenous reptile.

A rodent rode on a rickety, red river raft.

The runner reached for a rubbery rope to rescue the red robin on the rough round roof.

The reliable robot repaired a rigid rivet and removed the rocket's rusty rod.

Edith Namm

Sam saved a sample of the salty sandy salad.

Scott scattered sixty-six sticky sticks.

Did Shay say he saw a sharp saw?
If Shay said he saw a sharp saw, where's the sharp saw that Shay said he saw?

Spray the spry spruce standing near the shady, shabby shacks.

Shawn says he sheared the shorn sheep with sharpened shears.
If Shawn sheared the shorn sheep with sharpened shears, where's the shorn sheep Shawn sheared?

Six squirrels squirted six squeamish squids.

Stanley startled a strong, stately steed standing on a sturdy, stony stand.

The skunk's strong scent sent seven students scrambling.

Sue said she saw six slim snakes swing and sway to swing song sounds.

A seafaring sailor sold seventy-seven salty salmon.

Edith Namm

Stanley stripped the striped strip's stripes.

Steve stumbled over a stark, stubby stump.

The stunning stylish suite suited the suave, svelte suitor.

Spencer spent a sunny, sultry summer swimming in the shady, shallow stream.

Sadie said she saw the summer sun shining on a single, silent, serene swan swimming in a shallow stream.

The sunny site was a sight for sore eyes.

Sheila shook six skimply, shriveled shrubs.

Stacey slipped on the slick, slippery, slushy, snowy street.

Sam snatched seven sour snacks from Scott's soggy, snazzy sack.

A seagull soared while a scholar scored.

A slithery, striped snake snapped at a skinny, silver snapper.

Sy sighted sixty-six small snails swimming in the sea.
If Sy sighted sixty-six small snails swimming in the sea, where's the sixty-six small snails Sy sighted?

Troy's thoughtful teacher toasted Troy's triumphant team.

Theo thinks the thirty-three thinkers thought thoughtful thoughts.

Ten testy testers tested ten tense teens.

Two tired teens took turns trimming the tangled tags on thirty-three thick towels.

Thirty trembling teenagers took ten tough tests.

Thirsty Theo tasted thirty tasty tangy tangerines.
If thirsty Theo tasted thirty tasty tangy tangerines, where are the thirty tasty tangy tangerines that thirsty Theo tasted?

It's time for Tim to thyme the three turkeys.

Ten, tame, tan tigers tenderly touched twenty tiny, timid, tired turtles.

Tom was not taught to tie a taut knot.

Tucker tied twenty thick twigs with thick twine.

Did the upholsterer upholster the unique upholstery? If the upholsterer upholstered the unique upholstery, where's the unique upholstery that the upholsterer upholstered?

The umpire's uncle undertook to use an unfamiliar unique unicycle.

The uptight umpire uttered umpteen ultimatums.

The unanimous decision to wear uniforms unified the union.

Vic visited various, vast, valuable valley vacancies.

Vera veered away from a venomous viper.

The vocal village voter verified his vote.

The visionary visualized a valid victory for the valiant villagers.

Vivacious Vicky vows that valuable, valid, vital vitamins give her vim, vigor, and vitality.

Which wish do you wish to switch?

Will Wright will write which way the witty writer went.

Which witch was wistfully whisked westward?

When will Willy welcome the wise western women winners?

Wanda wishes the windy, wintry weather would wander westward.

The wealthy, worldly women wondered whether the wiry whippet would win.

The watchful waiter waited while Walter waddled to the widened wooden wharf.

The wrinkled walrus wallowed in the warm water.

The wary warbler watched the weak wasp wavering on the white wall.

Did Wendy write about the Wonders of the World?
If Wendy wrote about the Wonders of the World, where are the Wonders that Wendy wrote about?

Edith Namm

The willowy willow wilted and withered.

Was Will willing to widen the weak white wall?

Would Woody want to wake and wash the whopping, wobbly whale?

Wayne waits for a way to have four weights weighed.

If you could, would you have wound bandage around the wound?

Did William whittle a wooden whistle?
If William whittled a wooden whistle, where is the wooden whistle that William whittled?

Was the xylophonist or the xylophonist's xylophone x-rayed?

The young yapping yak yearned for yummy, yellow yams and yolks.

Can yoga make you yearn to yawn?

Did the young yeoman yank a yellow yo-yo from the youth on the yellow yacht?
If the young yeoman yanked a yellow yo-yo from the youth on the yellow yacht, where's the yellow yo-yo that the yeoman yanked?

Zeke zoomed in on a zillion, zany zebras zig-zagging in the zoo zone.

Zack zestfully zipped a zillion zippy zippers.

Zoe zealously zeroed in the zeroes in her zonal address.

Rhyming Riddles and Tons of Tongue Twisters for Miles of Smiles

OTHER BOOKS WRITTEN BY EDITH NAMM, M.A., C.S.G.

Available at the following Web Sites:

http://www.1stbooks.com (start with the number 1)

http://www.amazon.com

http://www.bn.com (Barnes and Noble)

http://www.borders.com

THE WRITE WAY TO POSITIVE PARENTING

Learn what can empower a Parent and Child to experience a Sense of Well-Being and successfully cope with the stress of Daily Living.
Discover:
How to recognize the signs of Anger, Resentment, Fear and Depression in One's Behavior and Handwriting.
The Write Way to handle Emotional Stress.
The Basics for Satisfying Parent/Child Relationships.
The ABC's for Positive Thoughts and Actions.
The Handwriting Exercises that can empower One to feel comfortable, confident and fulfilled.

LEARNING TO SEE WHAT A CHILD'S HANDWRITING SHOWS AND TELLS

A RESOURCE MANUAL for Educators, Counselors, and Psychologists that presents the basic concepts of Handwriting Analysis that can help to accurately and objectively evaluate a Child's Emotional Growth and Energy Level.

Discover:

How to identify Childhood Fears and the Defense Strategies a Child uses to deal with his/her real or imagined Fears.

How to recognize the signs of Anger and Depression in a Child's Handwriting.

How to identify a Child's Learning Style for processing information.

The Handwritten exercises that can empower a Preteen/Adolescent to feel confident, socially comfortable, and successfully cope with the Stress of Daily Living.

Rhyming Riddles and Tons of Tongue Twisters for Miles of Smiles

THE WINNING WAYS TO RELIEVE STRESS AND INCREASE POSITIVE ENERGY POWER (PEP)

A STRESS MANAGEMENT GUIDE that shows how Food, Color, and Specialized Handwriting Exercises can empower One to successfully cope with the Stress of Daily Living.

Discover:

How to recognize signs of Anger, Resentment, Fear and Depression in One's Behavior and Handwriting.

The Write Way to handle Emotional Stress.

The Basics for Satisfying Relationships.

How to effectively relieve Emotional Stress by accentuating the Positive Energy of Color in One's Surroundings, in the food One eats, and in the Clothes One wears.

Edith Namm

THE WRITE WAY TO GO FROM STRESS TO SERENITY AND TONS OF TONGUE TWISTERS FOR MILES OF SMILES

Dedicated to all those whose lives are touched by Cancer
Learn what it takes to reduce One's Emotional Stress, and Positively Energize One's Mind, Body, and Spirit.
Discover:
How to recognize the signs of Anger, Resentment, and Sadness in One's Handwriting.
The Write Way to relieve Feelings of Anger, Anxiety, and Sadness.
How Emotional Stress affects all the Body Systems.
The Writing Exercise that can raise One's level of Self-Confidence.
The Write Way to a Positive Self Image and Belief System.
How to Laugh One's way to Good Health.

About The Author

EDITH NAMM is both an Educator and a Specialized Handwriting Analyst. She holds a Master's Degree in Guidance from New York University and was certified as a Specialized Graphoanalyst by the Institute of Graphological Science in Dallas, Texas.

EDITH NAMM has 25 years of experience as a Guidance Counselor with the New York City Board of Education and in 1986 was honored as "The Outstanding Guidance Counselor" in District 21, Brooklyn.

She has 12 years of experience as a Certified Specialized Graphoanalyst.

EDITH NAMM is the Author of 4 other books:

The Write Way To Positive Parenting
Learning To See What A Child's Handwriting Shows And Tells
The Winning Ways To Relieve Stress And Increase Positive Energy Power (Pep)
The Write Way To Go From Stress To Serenity

Printed in the United Kingdom
by Lightning Source UK Ltd.
121342UK00003B/100/A